TH

COMPLETE

VEGETARIAN

DIABETIC

COOKBOOK

FOR

BEGINNERS

Simple, Fast and Delicious
Homemade Vegetarian Diabetic
Recipes for the Newly Diagnosed
with 28-Day Meal Plan for Healthy
Living.

ROSIE TIM

i

Table of Contents

Introduction

Diabetes can be managed with the aid of food. It has several health benefits, including supplying your body with essential nutrients and preventing blood sugar spikes.

A vegetarian diet entails avoiding all forms of meat in your meals. It provides you with natural health advantages and lowers your risk of type 2 diabetes and the medical complications linked to it. You can try a variety of nutritious vegetarian recipes to reduce your carb intake and regulate your blood sugar levels. Discover delicious and healthy vegetarian recipes for diabetics by reading this blog.

High blood sugar levels are a symptom of the lifestyle disorder known as diabetes. If you don't control your blood sugar levels, it can cause serious health issues. Your diet is extremely important in managing diabetes, in addition to physical activity and establishing a healthy lifestyle routine. It's good news that you can better manage your diabetes if you're a vegetarian. Vegetarian food contains more nutrients and fewer calories, which can help you control your blood sugar levels.

Why Is It Necessary to Change to a Plant-Based Diet?

Fruits, vegetables, and nuts in particular are especially helpful in treating a number of chronic diseases. They aid in lowering cholesterol levels, slowing the progression of cancer, and preventing type 2 diabetes. Foods made from plants are high in fiber, phytochemicals, antioxidants, and folate. They are all advantageous to general health. To maintain your weight, it's imperative to pay attention to the portion sizes of foods high in fat. The ideal at-home treatment for diabetic patients is a vegetarian diet.

Minerals and other nutrients for the body are abundant in vegetables. Including vegetables in your meals can help you stay healthy and keep your blood sugar levels in check. They have a high fiber content, which reduces how quickly your body absorbs glucose. Consult a dietician to learn which vegetables are best for diabetics.

People with type-2 diabetes can maintain good health while consuming a variety of vegetarian meals by eating a lot of vegetables. The following vegetables are the best for those with type 2 diabetes:

1. Low-glycemic-index vegetables

The ranking system is based on the glycemic index. How quickly the body absorbs glucose from the food is indicated by the GI rating of the food. Compared to foods with a low glycemic index, foods with a high glycemic index absorb glucose more quickly. Green beans, cauliflower, broccoli, tomato, spinach, and brinjal are examples of vegetables with low glycemic indexes.

2. Vegetables with High Fiber Content

Vegetables with high fiber content are crucial for diabetics following a vegetarian diet. Fiber aids in maintaining cholesterol levels and reducing constipation. It also aids in weight control. Carrots, beets, split peas, sprouts, and broccoli are vegetables with high fiber content.

3. Produce high in protein

The building blocks of muscles are proteins. It is one of the body's essential nutrients as a result. For diabetics, protein-rich foods keep you feeling full for a very long time. It lessens the desire to snack in between meals. As a result, it lowers your carbohydrate intake and aids in blood sugar regulation. Compared to other vegetables, spinach, broccoli, cauliflower, bell peppers, and mushrooms have higher protein contents.

4. High Nitrate Content

Natural nitrate lowers blood pressure and promotes the health of the circulatory system. Eat vegetables that naturally contain nitrates rather than foods that have been artificially nitrated. Beetroot, lettuce, spinach, and mustard greens are a few examples of these vegetables. These vegetables can be a part of your diabetes diet plan.

Advantages of a Vegetarian Diet for Diabetes Patients

One of the best diets for diabetics is a vegetarian one. This kind of diet aids in lowering saturated fat consumption. As a result, it prevents your body's cholesterol levels from rising and lowers your risk of developing cardiovascular diseases. A vegetarian diet also regulates body weight, which is a significant factor that causes blood sugar levels to rise.

For diabetic patients, a vegetarian diet plan should include grains, fruits, nuts, and vegetables. It might give your body the essential nutrients it needs. As a result, it contributes to reducing the risk of contracting diseases like diabetes. A vegetarian diet has many health advantages, including lowering blood pressure, cholesterol, and the risk of heart disease. The following are some additional advantages of a vegetarian diet for diabetics:

➤ Less consumption of saturated fat

 Food items derived from animal sources naturally contain saturated fats. As a result, non-vegetarians consume more saturated fats, which raises the risk of high cholesterol. In place of meat and poultry, vegetarians eat less food containing saturated fats, such as cheese, nuts, legumes, or eggs. Sources of plant-based protein aid in the control of diabetes and heart health.

> Better weight management

The majority of the foods in a vegetarian diet come from plants. They are low in calories and high in fiber. Increased consumption of plant-based foods (instead of foods high in calories) aids in lowering daily calorie intake. In the end, it contributes to maintaining a healthy body weight.

SIMPLE VEGETARIAN DIABETIC RECIPES, INGREDIENTS AND PREPARATIONS

Even though diabetic meals are similar to other meals, they contain ingredients high in fiber and low in carbohydrates. Therefore, diabetic recipes aid in controlling blood sugar levels. Diabetes patients can try any number of vegetarian and healthy recipes. There are many vegetarian recipes for diabetes that are high in fiber and low in carbohydrates. You can use these recipes for smoothies and desserts as well as for breakfast, lunch, and dinner.

Farro Salad with Arugula, Artichokes & Pistachios

The use of farro that has already been cooked reduces the amount of time needed to prepare this dish. And you can make it in the same bowl that you serve it in, which cuts down on the amount of dishes you have to wash.

Total Time: Twenty minutes

Servings: One

Ingredients

- One tablespoon lemon juice
- One tablespoon extra-virgin olive oil
- Two tablespoons pomegranate seeds (arils) or dried cranberries
- ¾ cup cooked farro
- Two cups packed baby arugula
- Two tablespoons thinly sliced fresh basil

- ¼ cup packed small fresh mint leaves
- 1/8 teaspoon salt
- One canned whole artichoke heart (or 4 quarters), rinsed and chopped
- ¾ ounce soft goat cheese, crumbled (2 Tbsp.)
- Two tablespoons chopped salted dry-roasted pistachios

Directions

- ❖ In a salad bowl, whisk together the lemon juice and oil.
- ❖ Mix in the artichoke hearts, farro, arugula, mint, and basil.
- ❖ Season with salt. Goat cheese, pistachios, and pomegranate seeds should be sprinkled over the top.

Mushroom & Tofu Stir-Fry

This tofu and vegetable stir-fry is both speedy and simple to prepare, making it an excellent option for a weeknight meal. Tofu that has been baked develops a firm, meaty texture that crisps up wonderfully when placed in a hot pan. You can find it in flavors such as teriyaki and sesame, both of which are delicious here. You can also find it in other flavors. You could also go for the smoked variety, which maintains the same consistency but has a more robust flavor. Place atop a bed of brown rice.

Total Time: Twenty minutes

Servings: Five

Ingredients

- Four tablespoons peanut oil or canola oil, divided
- One bunch scallions, trimmed and cut into 2-inch pieces
- One medium red bell pepper, diced
- One large clove garlic, grated
- One pound mixed mushrooms, sliced
- One tablespoon grated fresh ginger
- One (8 ounce) container baked tofu or smoked tofu, diced
- Three tablespoons oyster sauce or vegetarian oyster sauce

Directions

- ❖ Over high heat, bring two tablespoons of oil to a boil in a large cast-iron skillet or wok with a flat bottom.
- ❖ After adding the mushrooms and bell pepper, continue to cook the mixture for about 4 minutes, stirring it occasionally to ensure even cooking.
- ❖ Cook for an additional thirty seconds after stirring in the scallions, ginger, and garlic. Place the vegetables in a bowl for later use.
- ❖ To the skillet, add the remaining 2 tablespoons of oil along with the cubes of tofu. Cook for three to

four minutes, turning once, until the meat is browned.

❖ Combine the vegetables and oyster sauce by stirring them together. Cook while stirring for about a minute, or until the mixture is hot.

Easy Pea & Spinach Carbonara

Because fresh pasta takes less time to prepare than dried, it is an indispensable ingredient for speedy weeknight meals like this one, which is good for you. The smooth sauce has a foundation of egg as its primary ingredient. Because they do not get fully cooked, you should use eggs that have been pasteurized while still in the shell if that is your preference.

Total Time: Twenty minutes

Servings: Four

Ingredients

- Two tablespoons extra-virgin olive oil
- Half cup panko breadcrumbs, preferably whole-wheat
- One small clove garlic, minced
- Eight tablespoons grated Parmesan cheese, divided
- One (9 ounce) package fresh tagliatelle or linguine
- Three large egg yolks

- Three tablespoons finely chopped fresh parsley
- One large egg
- Half teaspoon ground pepper
- ¼ teaspoon salt
- Eight cups baby spinach
- One cup peas (fresh or frozen)

Directions

- ❖ A large pot should have ten cups of water added to it, which should then be brought to a boil over high heat.
- ❖ While that is going on, bring the oil to a simmer in a large skillet set over medium-high heat. After adding the breadcrumbs and the garlic, continue to cook the mixture for about two minutes

while stirring it frequently. After transferring to a smaller bowl, stir in 2 tablespoons of grated Parmesan cheese and the chopped parsley. Set aside.

- ❖ In a medium bowl, use a whisk to combine the remaining 6 tablespoons of Parmesan, the egg yolks, the egg, pepper, and salt.
- ❖ For one minute, while stirring it occasionally, cook the pasta in water that is already boiling. After adding the spinach and peas, continue cooking the pasta for one additional minute, or until it reaches the desired tenderness. Keep aside a quarter cup of the cooking liquid. After draining, place the food in a large bowl.

- ❖ Mix the reserved cooking water into the egg mixture in a slow, steady stream. Toss the pasta with a pair of tongs as you gradually add the sauce mixture to the pasta.
- ❖ Serve topped with the breadcrumb mixture that was reserved earlier.

Winter Greens Bowl

Beans and quinoa contribute a ton of flavor and plant-based protein to this dish, which is finished off with a tangy and creamy lemon-garlic dressing. This meal can be prepared in just one pan.

Ingredients

Greens Bowl

- Half cup quinoa
- One medium head cauliflower, cut into florets
- One cup low-sodium vegetable broth
- One (15 ounce) can no-salt-added cannellini beans: rinsed
- ¼ teaspoon salt
- Four cups chopped kale
- Half cup chopped walnuts (toasted)

Dressing

- ❖ ¾ cup whole-milk plain Greek yogurt
- ❖ Three tablespoons water
- ❖ One tablespoon extra-virgin olive oil
- ❖ One clove garlic, minced
- ❖ Two teaspoons cider vinegar
- ❖ One teaspoon lemon zest
- ❖ Two tablespoons lemon juice
- ❖ Half teaspoon ground turmeric
- ❖ ¼ teaspoon salt
- ❖ ¼ teaspoon ground pepper

Directions

- ❖ To make a greens bowl, fill a large saucepan with about an inch and a half of water and outfit it with a steamer basket.

- ❖ Add the cauliflower, then place the pot over high heat and bring to a boil. Cover and steam for about 5 minutes, or until the meat is tender.
- ❖ Place the cauliflower in a large bowl, cover it, and place it in the oven to keep warm. Put the water in the trash.
- ❖ The next step is to bring the broth, quinoa, and salt to a boil in the pan. Put the heat on low, cover the pan, and wait for five minutes.
- ❖ After stirring in the kale and beans, continue cooking the quinoa for 5 to 8 minutes, or until it has absorbed all of the liquid. After adding the cauliflower, take the pan off the heat and cover it.

- ❖ To make the dressing, get a small bowl and whisk in the yogurt, water, oil, garlic, vinegar, lemon zest, lemon juice, turmeric, and a pinch each of salt and pepper until the ingredients are thoroughly combined.
- ❖ The dressing should be drizzled over the quinoa mixture, and the walnuts should be sprinkled on top.

Toloache (Chickpea Curry)

This chickpea curry is an authentic dish from India that can be prepared in a matter of minutes and is both quick and healthy to make thanks to the use of beans that have been canned for convenience. If you would like an additional serving of vegetables, you can mix in some florets of roasted cauliflower. You can serve this dish with warm naan or brown basmati rice.

Total Time: Fifteen minutes

Servings: Six

Ingredients

- One medium serrano pepper, cut into thirds
- Four large cloves garlic
- One 2-inch piece fresh ginger, peeled and coarsely chopped
- Two teaspoons ground coriander

- Two teaspoons ground cumin
- One medium yellow onion, chopped (1-inch)
- Six tablespoons canola oil or grapeseed oil
- kosher salt (3/4 teaspoon)
- Half teaspoon ground turmeric
- Three cups no-salt-added canned diced tomatoes with their juice (from a 28-ounce can)
- Two 15-ounce cans chickpeas, rinsed
- Two teaspoons garam masala
- Fresh cilantro for garnish

Directions

❖ In a food processor, chop the serrano pepper, garlic, and ginger until the ingredients are finely minced. After scraping down the sides, pulse the mixture once more. Add the onion and pulse it until it is finely chopped but not completely liquidized.

❖ In a large saucepan, bring the oil to a simmer over medium-high heat. After adding the onion mixture, continue to cook it for 3 to 5 minutes while stirring it occasionally until it has softened. After adding the coriander, cumin, and turmeric, continue cooking for another two minutes while stirring.

❖ Tomatoes should be processed in the food processor until they are chopped very finely. Salt should also be added to the pan at this point.

- ❖ Cook for four minutes, stirring the mixture occasionally, while the heat is reduced to maintain a simmer.
- ❖ After adding the chickpeas and garam masala, lower the heat to maintain a gentle simmer, cover the pot, and continue cooking for another 5 minutes while stirring occasionally. If desired, serve with cilantro sprinkled on top.

Blueberry and Edamame Dressing on a Salad of Kale and Avocado

This salad, which takes its inspiration from California, is packed to the brim with nutrient-dense produce and is a delicious and satiating way to get your daily dose of vitamins. The unusual trio of blueberries, edamame, and goat cheese is one that we really enjoy eating together.

Total Time: Twenty minutes

Servings: Four

Ingredients

- Six cups stemmed and coarsely chopped curly kale
- One avocado, diced

- One cup blueberries
- One cup halved yellow cherry tomatoes
- One cup cooked shelled edamame
- ¼ cup sliced almonds, toasted (see Tip)
- Half cup crumbled goat cheese (2 ounces)
- ¼ cup olive oil
- Three tablespoons lemon juice
- One tablespoon minced chives
- Two teaspoons honey
- One teaspoon Dijon mustard
- One teaspoon salt

Directions

- ❖ Place the kale in a large bowl and massage the leaves with your hands to loosen the kale's texture.

Combine the goat cheese, avocado, blueberries, tomatoes, edamame, and almonds in a bowl.

❖ In a small bowl or jar with a lid that fits tightly, combine the honey, mustard, chives, honey, and salt. The small bowl or jar can also be used. Whisk or shake it up really well.

❖ The salad should be tossed with the vinaigrette after it has been drizzled over it.

Zucchini-Chickpea Veggie Burgers with Tahini-Ranch Sauce

This recipe for vegan burgers is one that you will want to make time and time again. For a satisfying and nutritious homemade veggie burger, savory chickpea and zucchini patties are topped with a creamy, herb-flecked tahini ranch sauce, juicy tomato slices, and peppery arugula. Put them on buns or stuff them in pitas and serve them. I strongly advise you to make an additional portion of the sauce because it works wonderfully as a dip for vegetable sticks and as a wonderful salad dressing after being diluted with some water.

Total Time: Twenty five minutes

Servings: Four

Ingredients

- Four tablespoons tahini, divided

- One tablespoon lemon juice
- Three teaspoons white miso, divided
- Two teaspoons onion powder, divided
- Two teaspoons garlic powder, divided
- Two teaspoons ground pepper, divided
- One tablespoon extra-virgin olive oil
- One teaspoon chopped fresh chives plus 2 tablespoons, divided
- One cup packed fresh arugula
- One (15 ounce) can no-salt-added chickpeas, rinsed
- One teaspoon ground cumin
- ¼ teaspoon salt
- 1/3 cup old-fashioned rolled oats

- Fresh parsley leaves (¼ Cup)
- Half cup shredded zucchini
- Two tablespoons water
- Four whole-grain hamburger buns, toasted
- Four slices tomato

Directions

- ❖ In a small bowl, mix together 2 tablespoons of tahini, lemon juice, 1 teaspoon of miso, 1/4 teaspoon of garlic powder, 1/2 teaspoon of onion powder, and 1/4 teaspoon of black pepper. While continuing to whisk, gradually add water until you have a homogenous mixture. Mix in one teaspoon of chopped chives. Set aside.

- ❖ In a food processor, combine the chickpeas, cumin, salt, the two additional tablespoons of tahini, the two teaspoons of miso, one teaspoon of garlic powder, one teaspoon of pepper, and three-quarters of a teaspoon of onion powder.

❖ Pulse the ingredients, pausing the process once or twice to scrape down the sides, until a coarse mixture is formed that can be pressed together without falling apart. Add the parsley and the additional 2 tablespoons of chives, and pulse the mixture until the herbs are finely chopped and incorporated throughout the dish. Place in a bowl for serving.

❖ To remove any excess moisture from the zucchini, simply squeeze it in a clean kitchen towel. To the chickpea mixture, add the zucchini, and using your hands, combine the ingredients while pressing them together to mash them up. Form into 4 patties.

❖ Warm the oil in a large nonstick skillet by keeping the heat at medium-high. After adding the patties, continue cooking for another 4 to 5 minutes, or until the patties are golden and beginning to crisp. Flip with caution and continue cooking until.

❖ Place the burgers on buns and top them with the tahini ranch sauce, arugula, and tomato slices before serving.

Potatoes stuffed with salsa and black beans.

With this straightforward recipe for loaded baked potatoes with salsa, beans, and avocado, taco night can easily be transformed into baked potato night. Even on the busiest of weeknights, you'll have time to prepare this quick and simple meal for the whole family because it only requires ten minutes of hands-on preparation time. When made with sweet potatoes instead of russet potatoes, this dish is every bit as satisfying.

Total Time: Twenty five minutes

Servings: Four

Ingredients

- Four medium russet potatoes
- Half cup fresh salsa
- One ripe avocado, sliced
- One (15 ounce) can pinto beans, rinsed, warmed and lightly mashed
- Four teaspoons chopped pickled jalapeños

Directions

- ❖ Fork holes should be made in potatoes all over. Microwave on Medium for approximately 20 minutes, turning once or twice to ensure even cooking. (Another option is to bake the potatoes at

425 degrees Fahrenheit until they are tender, which should take anywhere from 45 minutes to 1 hour.)

- ❖ Transfer the potatoes to a clean cutting board and allow them to slightly cool down.

- ❖ Make a cut down the length of the potato to open it, but stop short of cutting all the way through. This will protect your hands. Hold the potatoes in a kitchen towel. Pinch the ends so that the flesh is exposed.

- ❖ Add some salsa, avocado, black beans, and jalapenos to the top of each potato. Warmly serve.

Buttermilk Fried Tofu with Smoky Collard Greens

The crispiness of the pan-fried tofu that results from dipping it in buttermilk first produces an effect similar to that of fried chicken. While maintaining its status as a vegetarian dish, the collard greens can be given a smoky flavor by seasoning them with paprika. The preparation of this quick, easy, and nutritious dinner takes only 25 minutes, making it an excellent choice for evenings during the busy workweek.

Total Time: Twenty minutes

Servings: Four

Ingredients

- Six tablespoons grapeseed oil or canola oil, divided
- One (1 pound) package chopped collards
- Half cup water
- One tablespoon cider vinegar
- Half teaspoon smoked paprika
- ¾ teaspoon salt, divided
- One (14 to 16 ounce) package extra-firm tofu, drained
- One cup buttermilk
- Half teaspoon garlic powder
- Half teaspoon onion powder
- ¼ teaspoon cayenne pepper
- One cup whole-wheat panko
- Hot (spicy) honey for serving

Directions

❖ In a large saucepan, bring one tablespoon of oil up to temperature over medium heat. After adding the collards and the water, cook them for about 8 minutes, covered, while stirring them occasionally, until they are soft and wilted. Take the pan off the heat and add the vinegar, paprika, and a half teaspoon of salt, stirring constantly. Cover to keep warm.

❖ In the meantime, cut the block of tofu lengthwise into eight equal pieces. Use paper towels to blot in order to remove any excess water. In a baking dish that is 7 inches by 11 inches, whisk together buttermilk, garlic powder, onion powder, and cayenne. After adding the tofu, turn it to coat it evenly. Allow to stand for five minutes while turning once.

- ❖ Put some panko bread crumbs on a plate. Panko should be used to coat both sides of the tofu after it has been dredged.
- ❖ In a large nonstick skillet, bring three tablespoons of oil up to temperature over medium-high heat.
- ❖ After adding the tofu, cook it for about 4 to 5 minutes, or until it is golden brown and crispy on one side. After you have flipped the tofu, drizzle the remaining 2 tablespoons of oil over it.

- ❖ Continue cooking for approximately 4 minutes more, or until the other side is browned.
- ❖ To serve, sprinkle the remaining 1/4 teaspoon of salt over the tofu and, if desired, accompany it with some hot honey and collard greens.

Open-Face Goat Cheese Sandwich with Tomato & Avocado Salad

This quick and easy lunch can be prepared in just 10 minutes, making it an excellent choice for times when you are pressed for time.

Total Time: Ten minutes

Servings: Four

Ingredients

- ¾ cup grape tomatoes, halved
- 1/3 avocado, peeled and cubed (or sliced)
- 1/8 teaspoon salt
- ¼ cup chopped fresh basil plus 2 Tbsp., divided
- ¾ ounce soft goat cheese (2 Tbsp.)
- One large slice whole-wheat bread (1 1/2 oz.), toasted
- 1/8 teaspoon ground pepper

- One tablespoon pine nuts, toasted (see Tip)
- Two teaspoons extra-virgin olive oil
- One tablespoon balsamic vinegar

Directions

- ❖ In a small bowl, combine the tomatoes, avocado, salt, and a quarter of a cup of the basil.
- ❖ Toast should be topped with goat cheese. Pepper and the remaining 2 tablespoons should be sprinkled on top. basil.
- ❖ Alongside the toast, serve the tomato salad in the bowl. Pine nuts should be sprinkled over everything, and oil should be drizzled over it. Vinegar should be served on the side.

Chickpea Green Goddess Salad with Green Goddess Dressing

A chickpea salad with cucumbers, tomatoes, and Swiss cheese is topped with a green goddess dressing that is made from avocado, buttermilk, and various herbs. The leftover dressing is delicious when served with vegetables that have been grilled.

Total Time: Fifteen minutes

Servings: Two

Ingredients

Dressing

- One avocado, peeled and pitted
- Two cups buttermilk
- ¼ cup chopped fresh herbs, such as tarragon, sorrel, mint, parsley and/or cilantro
- Two tablespoons rice vinegar
- Half teaspoon salt

Salad

- ❖ Three cups chopped romaine lettuce
- ❖ One cup sliced cucumber
- ❖ One (15 ounce) can chickpeas, rinsed
- ❖ ¼ cup diced low-fat Swiss cheese
- ❖ Six cherry tomatoes, halved if desired

Directions

- ❖ In order to make the dressing, fill a blender with avocado, buttermilk, herbs, vinegar, and salt. Blend until smooth. Blend to a silky smoothness.
- ❖ To make the salad, place the lettuce and cucumber in a bowl and toss them together with a quarter cup of the dressing.
- ❖ To finish, sprinkle some chickpeas, cheese, and tomatoes on top. (The extra dressing can be stored in the refrigerator for up to three days.

Summer Skillet Vegetable & Egg Scramble

Keep those fresh herbs and vegetables that are almost expired. They can be added to this vegetarian skillet egg scramble for a quick meal. Choose your favorite vegetables or use whatever you have on hand for this simple skillet recipe. Almost any vegetable will work.

Total Time: Thirty minutes

Servings: Four

Ingredients

- Two tablespoons olive oil
- Twelve ounces baby potatoes, thinly sliced

- Four cups thinly sliced vegetables, such as mushrooms, bell peppers, and/or zucchini (14 oz.)
- Three scallions, thinly sliced, green and white parts separated
- One teaspoon minced fresh herbs, such as rosemary or thyme
- Six large eggs (or 4 large eggs plus 4 egg whites), lightly beaten
- Two cups packed leafy greens, such as baby spinach or baby kale (2 oz.)
- Half teaspoon salt

Directions

❖ Over medium heat, warm oil in a sizable cast-iron or nonstick skillet. Add the potatoes; cover and cook for 8 minutes, stirring

frequently, until they start to
soften.

- ❖ Add the sliced vegetables and
  scallion whites; cook uncovered,
  stirring once or twice, for 8 to 10
  minutes, or until the vegetables
  are tender and just starting to
  brown.
- ❖ Stir in the herbs. Place the
  vegetable mixture around the
  pan's edge.
- ❖ Medium-low heat should be used.
  In the center of the pan, add the
  eggs and the scallion greens.
  About 2 minutes, while stirring,
  cook the eggs until they are softly
  scrambled.
- ❖ Add leafy greens to the eggs and
  stir. Removing from the heat and

thoroughly combining. Add salt and mix.

Mixed Greens with Lentils & Sliced Apple

This lentil, feta, and apple salad makes a filling vegetarian main dish that you can quickly prepare for lunch. Change to drained canned lentils to save time, but make sure to look for low-sodium varieties and give them a rinse before incorporating them into the salad.

Total Time: Ten minutes

Servings: One

Ingredients

- Two cups mixed salad greens
- Half cup cooked lentils
- One apple, cored and sliced, divided
- Two tablespoons crumbled feta cheese
- One tablespoon red-wine vinegar
- Two teaspoons extra-virgin olive oil

Directions

- ❖ Add lentils, about half the apple slices, and feta to the greens as a garnish.
- ❖ Add a vinegar and oil drizzle. The remaining apple slices should be served separately.

Salad of quinoa, avocado, and chickpeas Various Greens

This tangy and healthy salad recipe has staying power thanks to the protein-rich quinoa and chickpeas.

Total Time: Twenty five minutes

Servings: Two

Ingredients

- Water (2/3 cup)
- 1/3 cup quinoa
- ¼ teaspoon kosher salt or other coarse salt

- One clove garlic, crushed and peeled
- Two teaspoons grated lemon zest
- Three tablespoons lemon juice
- Three tablespoons olive oil
- ¼ teaspoon ground pepper
- One cup rinsed no-salt-added canned chickpeas
- One medium carrot, shredded (1/2 cup)
- One (5 ounce) package prewashed mixed greens, such as spring mix or baby kale-spinach blend (8 cups packed)

Directions

- ❖ In a tiny pan, bring water to a boil. Add quinoa and stir. Turn down the heat to low, cover the pan, and simmer for 15 minutes or until all the liquid has been absorbed. Fluff and separate the grains with a fork; allow to cool for five minutes.

❖ In the interim, salt the garlic on the cutting board. Use the side of a spoon to smash the garlic until a paste forms. into a medium bowl, scrape.

❖ Add pepper, oil, lemon juice, and zest to the mixture. 3 Tbsp. of the dressing should be transferred to a small bowl and set aside.

❖ The remaining dressing should be added to the bowl along with the chickpeas, carrot, and avocado. Gently toss to combine. To allow flavors to meld, allow to stand for

5 minutes. Toss the quinoa gently to coat after adding it.

❖ In a large bowl, combine the greens with the 3 Tbsp. dressing that was set aside. Place the greens on two plates, then add the quinoa mixture on top.

Hummus and Veggie Sandwich

The ideal vegetarian lunch on-the-go is this mile-high sandwich with hummus and vegetables. Depending on your mood, mix it up with various hummus flavors and vegetables of various kinds.

Total Time: Ten minutes

Servings: One

Ingredients

- Two slices whole-grain bread
- Three tablespoons hummus
- ¼ avocado, mashed
- Half cup mixed salad greens
- ¼ medium red bell pepper, sliced
- ¼ cup sliced cucumber
- ¼ cup shredded carrot

Directions

- ❖ Spread hummus on one slice of bread and avocado on the other.
- ❖ Add greens, bell pepper, cucumber, and carrot to the

sandwich. Cut in half, then
present.

No-Cook Salad of black beans

For picnics and potlucks, a traditional
black bean salad is a must-have dish.
The avocado has been blended to give
this vegan version its creaminess. Any
combination of salad greens will do, but
if you want to give this hearty salad a
peppery kick, try arugula.

Total Time: Thirty minutes

Servings: Four

Ingredients

- Half cup thinly sliced red onion
- One medium ripe avocado, pitted and roughly chopped
- ¼ cup cilantro leaves
- ¼ cup lime juice
- Two tablespoons extra-virgin olive oil
- One clove garlic, minced
- Half teaspoon salt
- Eight cups mixed salad greens
- Two medium ears corn, kernels removed, or 2 cups frozen corn, thawed and patted dry
- One pint grape tomatoes, halved
- One (15 ounce) can black beans, rinsed

Directions

- ❖ In a medium bowl, add the onion and then the cold water.
- ❖ Place aside. In a small food processor, combine the avocado, cilantro, lime juice, oil, garlic, and salt. Process until creamy and smooth, stopping to scrape down the sides as necessary.
- ❖ Salad greens, corn, tomatoes, and beans should all be combined in a big bowl just before serving. Add the avocado dressing and the drained onions to the bowl. Toss to coat

Black-bean and sweet potato burgers

These curry-flavored vegan sweet potato-black bean burgers are simple to make. A cast-iron pan is used to cook the outside, which becomes crispy after the mixture is blended with your hands to create a soft, uniform texture. Use gluten-free oats and serve the patty in a lettuce wrap without the bun to convert this dish to gluten-free status as well.

Total Time: Forty five minutes

Servings: Four

Ingredients

- Two cups grated sweet potato
- Half cup old-fashioned rolled oats

- One cup no-salt-added black beans, rinsed
- Half cup chopped scallions
- ¼ cup vegan mayonnaise
- One tablespoon no-salt-added tomato paste
- One teaspoon curry powder
- 1/8 teaspoon salt
- Half cup plain unsweetened almond milk yogurt
- Two tablespoons chopped fresh dill
- Two tablespoons lemon juice
- Two tablespoons extra-virgin olive oil
- Four whole-wheat hamburger buns, toasted
- One cup thinly sliced cucumber

Directions

- ❖ Place the grated sweet potato in a big bowl and squeeze out any extra moisture using paper towels. Oats should be ground to a fine powder in a food processor before being added to the sweet potato mixture.

- ❖ To the bowl, add the beans, scallions, mayonnaise, tomato paste, curry powder, and salt. Combine the ingredients with your hands. Four 1/2-inch-thick patties should be formed. The patties should be placed on a plate and chilled for 30 minutes.

- ❖ In a small bowl, combine yogurt, dill, and lemon juice; set aside.

- ❖ In a sizable cast-iron skillet, heat the oil over medium-high heat.

Add the patties and cook for three minutes on each side or until golden brown.

❖ Top and bottom bun halves should each receive an equal amount of yogurt sauce.

❖ Replace the top bun halves after adding a burger and some cucumber slices to each bottom bun half.

Roasted vegetable pizza

For those who have or don't have coeliac disease, making this gorgeous gluten-free pizza is a great idea.

Servings: Four

Total Time: 35 minutes

Ingredients

- 75g potatoes, peeled and chopped small
- 50g (chickpea) flour
- 125g ground rice
- 50g cornflour
- half teaspoon bicarbonate of soda
- half teaspoon cream of tartar
- 25g sunflower spread
- 125ml semi-skimmed milk
- a little oil for greasing

For the topping:

- 4 medium tomatoes, sliced
- half red pepper, sliced
- half yellow pepper, sliced
- one small red onion, sliced
- one small tin (290g) button mushrooms, drained and halved
- 40grams feta cheese, crumbled
- Handful fresh basil leaves, torn

Directions

- ❖ The potatoes should be added to a pan of boiling water and cooked for 15 minutes or until tender.
- ❖ Turn on the gas or oven to 220°C. Mix the gram flour, rice flour, corn flour, bicarbonate of soda, and cream of tartar in a sizable bowl.

- ❖ Spread until the mixture resembles breadcrumbs after adding the potato.
- ❖ Form a ball, add just enough milk to make a soft dough, roll out to a 30 cm diameter, and place on a baking sheet that has been lightly oiled.
- ❖ Add tomato slices, pepper and onion slices, and half of a mushroom as garnish.
- ❖ Place the feta crumbles on top and bake for 15 to 20 minutes, or until the vegetables are crisp-golden.
- ❖ Serve after scattering the basil.

Recipe advice

Add a few crushed garlic cloves to the potato to create a garlic crust.

Before adding the peppers, onion, and pepper slices to the tomato slices, add 1 teaspoon of dried organo and a pinch of red pepper flakes for flavor.

Kale and green lentil soup

A simple, quick-to-make, and incredibly healthy soup.

Servings: Four

Total time: Forty minutes

Ingredients

- Two teaspoon sunflower oil
- Two onions, finely chopped

- One large carrot, diced
- One stick celery, chopped
- One- two cloves garlic, crushed
- One teaspoon ground cumin
- One tablespoon tomato purée
- 1 x 400g can green lentils in water (add the water, too)
- 200g Cavolo Nero (black kale) or curly kale, chopped (thick stalks removed)
- 500ml vegetable stock
- black pepper, to taste

Directions

- ❖ The onions should be stirred in the oil for 7 to 10 minutes, or until they are well browned.

- ❖ Cook the carrot and celery for an additional two to three minutes while stirring frequently.
- ❖ Add the lentils, tomato purée, garlic, cumin, and mix thoroughly.
- ❖ After adding the stock, bringing it to a boil, lowering the heat, covering it, and gently simmering for 12 minutes.
- ❖ Replace the lid, add the kale, and simmer for an additional five minutes. Season with pepper and serve.

Recipe advice

Any stock, including chicken or beef, may be used. When possible, choose reduced-salt options for stock because it can contain a lot of salt.

Consider including shredded chicken breast or cubes of smoked or marinated tofu.

Other vegetables that you could include are peppers, courgettes, broccoli, or canned sweet corn.

Instructions for freezing: Freeze food in portions, then defrost in the refrigerator or microwave, stirring frequently.

Mediterranean pasta salad

This is a fantastic lunch option. It's a nice alternative to sandwiches with all the Mediterranean flavors.

Servings; Three

Total time: Thirty minutes

Ingredients

- 225g dried pasta shapes
- Ten cherry tomatoes, quartered
- Ten black olives, sliced
- Quarter cucumber, chopped
- Half red onion, thinly sliced
- 40g Feta cheese, crumbled
- 15g pine nuts, toasted
- One tablespoon olive oil
- One tablespoon balsamic vinegar
- Handful basil leaves

Directions

- ❖ Cook the pasta as directed on the package. Drain, then rinse with cold water.
- ❖ Serve the pasta after tossing it with the other ingredients.
- ❖ recipe advice
- ❖ Pine nuts can be toasted by placing them in a dry frying pan over medium heat, stirring frequently until they begin to turn brown, and then removing them from the pan right away to prevent further cooking.
- ❖ Use canned chickpeas in place of the pasta for a gluten-free variation.

Smoky tofu kebabs

a delectable meatless substitute for kebabs.

Servings: Four

Total Time: Forty Minutes

Ingredients

- 200g pack firm tofu, drained
- 2–3 medium courgettes, sliced thinly lengthways into 12 slices (300g)
- **For the marinade**
- Two tablespoon toasted coriander seeds

- One tablespoon toasted cumin seeds
- Four cloves garlic, peeled
- 4cm piece ginger, roughly chopped
- Two red chillies, deseeded and roughly chopped
- freshly ground black pepper
- one tablespoon sundried tomato purée
- three tablespoon white wine vinegar
- three tablespoon extra-virgin olive oil
- two tablespoon water

Directions

❖ Cut the tofu into 12 large cubes after thoroughly draining.

- ❖ Start by powdering the coriander and cumin seeds to make the marinade.

- ❖ Next, grind the garlic, ginger, and chillies into a rough paste in a mortar with a few generous pinches of pepper. Add the tomato purée, vinegar, olive oil, coriander, and cumin at this point. After that, stir in 2 tablespoons of water.

- ❖ Gently stir in the tofu after adding it to the marinade, cover it, and set it aside for at least one hour, preferably three to four. In two batches, microwave the clingfilm-wrapped courgette slices for 60 to 80 seconds, or until they are just soft enough to wrap around a piece of tofu without collapsing.

Alternately, blanch in boiling water for about 30 seconds and then thoroughly drain.

❖ Wrap strips of courgette around the tofu cubes just before cooking so that the courgette stays in place. Then slide the tofu onto skewers.

❖ Any remaining marinade in the bowl should be used to brush the courgette before grilling or barbecuing it for 10 to 15 minutes while turning it frequently.

Spinach, red onion and potato tortilla

This is ideal for lunch, a picnic, or a barbecue whether it is served warm or chilled.

Servings: Four

Total time: Forty five minutes

Ingredients

- 400g new potatoes
- 250g frozen leaf spinach (130g once defrosted and excess water squeezed out)
- One tablespoon olive oil
- One large red onion, thinly sliced
- Five eggs
- Pinch pepper, to season

Directions

- ❖ Depending on size, boil the potatoes in their skins for 15-20 minutes, or until almost done but still firm. To make them easier to handle, drain them and run them under a cold faucet before slicing each potato into slices that are 1/2 cm thick.

- ❖ Defrost the spinach in the meantime, squeeze out the extra liquid, and roughly chop it.
- ❖ A large nonstick frying pan with the oil added should be heated to medium. Cook the onion for two to three minutes, or until soft.
- ❖ In a bowl, whisk the eggs with the pepper, then add the spinach and potatoes.
- ❖ In the frying pan, pour the egg mixture. To make the tortilla into

an even shape, press the sides in and down with a spatula.

❖ The tortilla should be inverted onto a plate once it has nearly set (about 5 minutes), then slid back into the pan to cook the other side for 5 minutes. To ensure that the center of the tortilla is cooked, lower the heat and flip it twice more, cooking it for two to three minutes on each side.

❖ Place the tortilla on a plate and let it sit there for 10 to 15 minutes to cool. Serving it warm is ideal because it tastes much better. Allow to cool completely before slicing and packing for a packed lunch.

Recipe advice

❖ You can substitute other vegetables, such as peas and red pepper, for the spinach in this tortilla recipe (also known as a Spanish omelette). Or, try including some garlic or herbs.

Vegetarian chili

This adaptable dish is inexpensive and simple to prepare. It can be served with rice or baked sweet potatoes, wrapped with a salad, or turned into nachos, enchiladas, or tacos.

Servings: Eight

Total time: One hour

Ingredients

- Two teaspoon rapeseed oil
- 2-3 onions, finely chopped
- One red pepper, finely chopped
- 150g carrots, finely chopped
- One courgette, finely chopped
- 100g mushrooms, finely chopped
- One-two teaspoon chilli powder (mild or hot, according to your taste)
- One teaspoon ground cumin
- One teaspoon oregano
- 800g tin chopped tomatoes
- 400g tin lentils in unsalted water
- 400g tin cannellini beans in unsalted water
- One tablespoon omato ketchup
- coriander, to garnish

Directions

- ❖ The onions should be cooked for 5-8 minutes, depending on how large the pan is, until they begin to brown.
- ❖ Cook for an additional 10 minutes after adding the mushrooms, red pepper, carrots, and courgette.
- ❖ Add the tomatoes, cumin, oregano, and chili powder next. Mix thoroughly, then cook for an additional 10 minutes while stirring frequently.
- ❖ Add the beans, lentils, and ketchup along with their water. Mix thoroughly and bring to a low bubble. 30 minutes of gentle simmering with frequent stirring, with the lid on.

Recipe advice

- ❖ Frozen or kept in the refrigerator for up to three days.
- ❖ Be cautious when using chillies because you can always add more but never subtract them! Only add more if necessary after tasting it and giving the heat time to infuse.
- ❖ If you're serving it to friends, keep it mild and serve some chili sauce or flakes on the side so that everyone can add more heat if they'd like.

Instructions for freezing: Once cooked, suitable for freezing. Defrost in the refrigerator or microwave, then thoroughly reheat until everything is piping hot.

Burgers with black-eyed beans, feta, and herbs

A satisfying, protein-rich burger without meat.

Servings: Six

Total Time: One hour

Ingredients

- Two teaspoon olive oil
- Three spring onions, finely sliced
- 400grams tin black-eyed beans, drained and rinsed
- 75grams granary breadcrumbs

- 100grams feta cheese, crumbled
- Two tablespoon mixed fresh herbs, chopped
- One egg, beaten
- wholemeal rolls, to serve (4 x 70g)
- salad, red onions and tomato

Directions

- ❖ The spring onions should be fried for 1-2 minutes, or until softened, in a nonstick frying pan with half the oil heated.
- ❖ In a big bowl, mash the black-eyed beans with a fork. The remaining ingredients are then thoroughly mixed in.
- ❖ Six equal portions of the mixture should be formed into patties or burgers.

- ❖ Put on a baking sheet, brush with the leftover oil on each side, and chill for at least 30 minutes or until needed.
- ❖ Cook until thoroughly done on a medium barbecue or grill, 2-3 minutes per side.
- ❖ Green salad, tomatoes, and red onion are served inside a wholemeal roll.

Mushroom and bean enchiladas

A filling family meal that is inexpensive, simple to prepare, and healthy.

Servings: Four

Prep time: Thirty minutes

Ingredients

- Two teaspoon rapeseed oil
- Two onions, chopped
- Two cloves garlic, crushed
- One yellow pepper, chopped
- 1 x 400g tin chopped tomatoes
- 250g mushrooms, sliced
- Two-three chilli powder (mild or hot, to taste)
- One heaped tsp oregano

- One heaped tsp cumin
- Two tablespoon tomato puree
- 1 x 400g can green lentils
- One carrot, grated
- 1 x 400g can mixed beans, drained and rinsed
- 75grams reduced-fat Cheddar
- Four large wholemeal tortillas (approx. 65g each)
- 200grams low-fat yogurt

Directions

❖ Set the oven's temperature to 180°C/gas mark 4. In a saucepan with hot oil, cook the onion for two to three minutes, or until soft. Include the garlic, yellow pepper, mushrooms, cumin, oregano, and chili powder. The ingredients should be combined.

❖ Tomatoes, tomato puree, and carrot should be added. Mix well. Stirring occasionally, bring to a boil, reduce heat, cover with a lid, and simmer for 10 minutes.

❖ Mix in the green lentils and mixed beans before re-bringing the mixture to a boil. After stirring, turn off the heat.

❖ The bottom of a sizable ovenproof dish should be covered with 4 tablespoons of the chili mixture. Place the tortillas on a board, then distribute the remaining chili mixture among them. To seal, roll up the ends and fold them over.

They should be lined up in the ovenproof dish.

❖ Spread the enchiladas with a mixture of yogurt and grated Cheddar. Bake for 12 to 15 minutes, or until golden. with a side of salad.

Recipe advice

The chili mixture tastes great spooned over rice or baked sweet potatoes, or it can be used to make nachos that are better for you.

The chilli filling can be frozen as well.

You can substitute any herbs or spices you have in your spice cabinet in place of the ones we've listed in the ingredients.

Pad Thai

Noodles and vegetables stir-fried in a spicy, slightly sweet sauce.

Servings: Four

Total time: Thirty minutes

Ingredients

- 250grams dried rice noodles
- Two teaspoon rapeseed oil
- Six spring onions, chopped at angle in 1cm pieces
- Three cloves garlic, crushed
- 3cm fresh ginger, grated
- One Thai chilli, finely sliced
- One red pepper, finely chopped

- One courgette, cut into sticks
- 100grams frozen broad beans
- 100grams baby pak choi, leaves separated
- 200grams beansprouts
- 75grams canned pineapple in juice, drained, chopped small
- One tablespoon reduced-salt, gluten-free soy sauce
- juice one lime
- 15grams chopped coriander
- 50grams unsalted peanuts, roughly chopped and toasted
- One lime cut into wedges

Directions

- ❖ Noodles should be cooked for 3-5 minutes as directed on the package. Pour cold water over them, then drain and reserve.

- ❖ In a sizable skillet or wok, heat the oil. Stir-fry the spring onions for 3 minutes after adding them. Stir-fry the garlic, ginger, and chilli for an additional two minutes.

- ❖ After stirring-frying the red pepper and courgette for an additional minute, add the broad beans and pak choy. 1 minute of stirring.

- ❖ After 2 minutes of stirring, add the noodles, beansprouts, pineapple, soy sauce, and lime juice. Add the coriander after another 2 minutes of stirring.

- ❖ Place in a bowl and garnish with lime wedges and peanuts.

Recipe advice

Use a vegetable peeler to create ribbons out of a half a cucumber and serve as a side dish with lime juice and fresh coriander leaves.

Use soy beans in place of the broad beans or include some tofu to boost the amount of protein in this dish.

Sunomono (Japanese Cucumber Salad)

If you live close to an Asian market, you could use Japanese cucumbers instead of the English or slicing cucumbers used in this version of sunomono. We discovered that squeezing the cucumbers in paper towels removed enough excess moisture without adding more sodium, contrary to some recipes that call for salting the cucumbers first. This salad with Japanese influences is cool, crisp, and delicious.

Total Time: Fifteen minutes

Servings: Four

Cucumbers from hot houses or slicing cucumbers can be substituted for the Japanese cucumbers that are traditionally used to make sunomono. In this recipe, we call for slicing cucumbers, which have a crisp and flavorful flesh. We seed and partially peel slicing cucumbers before slicing them because they have tougher skin and larger seeds than other cucumber varieties. Sometime the term "seedless" is used to describe hot house cucumbers or English cucumbers. Although they frequently have smaller seeds that don't need to be removed, they do have seeds. They do not require peeling because they have skin that is thinner.

Ingredients

- Two medium cucumbers, or 1 large English cucumber
- ¼ cup rice vinegar
- One teaspoon sugar
- ¼ teaspoon salt
- Two tablespoons sesame seeds, toasted

Directions

- ❖ Cucumbers can be peeled to reveal alternating green stripes. Cut the cucumbers in half lengthwise, then use a spoon to remove the seeds. Slice very thinly using a sharp knife or a wide vegetable peeler. Use two layers of paper towels and gently squeeze to wring out any remaining moisture.
- ❖ In a medium bowl, mix the vinegar, sugar, and salt while stirring to combine. Mix well before adding the cucumbers and sesame seeds. Serve right away.

Strawberry-Chocolate Bark with Greek Yogurt

Fresh strawberries and chocolate chips are added to lightly sweetened Greek yogurt, which is then frozen so you can break it into pieces like chocolate bark (but healthier!). This vibrant snack or healthy dessert is ideal for both children and adults. To ensure the creamiest bark possible, use full-fat yogurt.

×

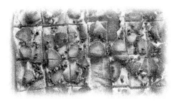

Total Time: Three hours

Servings: 32

Ingredients

- Three cups whole-milk plain Greek yogurt
- ¼ cup pure maple syrup or honey
- One teaspoon vanilla extract

- Two cups sliced strawberries
- ¼ cup mini chocolate chips

Directions

- ❖ Use parchment paper to line a baking sheet with a rim.
- ❖ In a medium bowl, combine yogurt, maple syrup (or honey), and vanilla. Spread into a 10- by 15-inch rectangle on the baking sheet that has been prepared.
- ❖ Add the strawberries and chocolate chips to the surface.
- ❖ Freeze for at least 3 hours, or until very firm. Cut or break into 32 pieces to serve.

Sautéd Zucchini and Mushrooms

Serve these straightforward turkey burgers with this side dish. Oregano and thyme are two additional fresh herbs that work well.

Total Time: Fifteen Minutes

Servings: Four

Ingredients

- Two teaspoons extra-virgin olive oil
- Two small zucchini, julienned
- Two cups sliced mushrooms
- Two teaspoons chopped fresh basil

- Salt & freshly ground pepper, to taste

Directions

❖ A big nonstick skillet with high heat is used to heat the oil. For 2 minutes, while stirring, add the zucchini.

❖ Cook, stirring, the basil and mushrooms for about a minute or until they are soft. Add salt and pepper to taste.

Root Vegetables Roasted in a Sheet Pan

You only need one pan to prepare an abundance of nourishing, tender, and vibrant root vegetables. Make a big batch of this recipe at the beginning of the week to use for quick, wholesome dinners all week.

Total Time: Fifty minutes

Servings: Eight

Ingredients

- Two large carrots
- Two medium parsnips, peeled
- Two medium beets, peeled
- One medium red onion
- One medium sweet potato
- Three tablespoons extra-virgin olive oil
- Two tablespoons apple cider vinegar or balsamic vinegar

- One tablespoon fresh herbs, such as thyme, rosemary or sage
- Half teaspoon kosher salt
- Half teaspoon ground pepper

Directions

- ❖ Oven rack placement and temperature adjustment to 425 degrees F. 2 large baking sheets should be lined with parchment paper.
- ❖ Slice carrots and parsnips on a diagonal into 1/2-inch-thick slices, then cut into half-moon shapes. Beets and onions should be cut into 1/2 inch thick wedges.
- ❖ Sweet potato should be cut into 3/4-inch cubes. About 12 cups of raw vegetables per day are recommended.

- ❖ In a big bowl, toss the vegetables with the oil, vinegar, herbs, salt, and pepper until well-coated. Spread each portion evenly among the prepared baking sheets.
- ❖ Roast the vegetables for 30 to 40 minutes, turning the pans top to bottom halfway through.

Easy Rice with Fried Cauliflower

In order to add more vegetables and reduce the amount of carbs, riced cauliflower is used in place of white or brown rice in this vegetarian version of fried rice. Fresh ginger adds a bright, warm bite and chile-garlic sauce amps up the heat. If the chile-garlic sauce's heat is too much for you, omit it and replace it with more tamari or soy sauce for a rich, fermented tang.

Total Time: Twenty five minutes

Servings: Four

Ingredients

- Two tablespoons peanut oil, divided
- Four large eggs, lightly beaten
- Four cups cauliflower rice (see Tip)
- One red bell pepper, chopped
- Two scallions, sliced, greens and whites separated, divided

- One tablespoon minced fresh ginger
- Two tablespoons chile-garlic sauce (such as sambal oelek)
- Two teaspoons reduced-sodium soy sauce or tamari
- Half cup unsalted peanuts

Directions

- ❖ In a sizable nonstick skillet, heat 1 tablespoon of oil over medium-high heat. Add eggs and cook for 1 1/2 to 2 minutes, tilting the pan and lifting the edges with a spatula to let the uncooked egg flow underneath.
- ❖ After flipping, cook for an additional 30 seconds or until the food is completely set. Place on a

cutting board and cut into strips that are suitable for eating.

❖ Over medium-high heat, preheat the remaining 1 tablespoon of oil in the pan. Add the ginger, bell pepper, scallion whites, and cauliflower rice.

❖ Cook for about 5 minutes, stirring occasionally, or until the cauliflower is soft and starting to brown.

❖ Add the eggs, peanuts, soy sauce (or tamari), and chili-garlic sauce. Stirring for 30 seconds or so, or until thoroughly combined and heated Add scallion greens to each serving as a garnish.

Zucchini

Simple Steaming This quick and simple method of cooking zucchini is also the most reliable. A quick few minutes of stovetop steaming will yield a nutritious vegetable side dish for dinner. Add some pesto for flavor by tossing.

Total Time: Ten minutes

Servings: Four

Ingredients

- Two pounds zucchini (about 4 medium), sliced 1/4 inch thick

Directions

- ❖ In a sizable saucepan with a steamer basket attached, bring 1 inch of water to a boil.
- ❖ Put in zucchini. Cover and steam for about 5 minutes, or until very tender.

Garlic Hummus

It's so simple to make this traditional hummus recipe—just throw a few ingredients in the food processor and pulse away! This healthy dip is extra smooth and creamy thanks to aquafaba, the liquid from a can of chickpeas. Serve with crudités, pita chips, or vegetable chips.

Total Time: Ten minutes

Servings: Eight

Ingredients

- One (15 ounce) can no-salt-added chickpeas
- ¼ cup tahini
- ¼ cup extra-virgin olive oil
- ¼ cup lemon juice
- One clove garlic
- One teaspoon ground cumin
- Half teaspoon chili powder
- Half teaspoon salt

Directions

- ❖ Chickpeas should be drained, saving 1/4 cup of the liquid. Add the chickpeas and the liquid you set aside to a food processor.
- ❖ Add the salt, tahini, oil, lemon juice, garlic, cumin, and chili powder. Puree for 2 to 3 minutes, or until very smooth.

Frittata with cheddar and zucchini

Cheddar cheese and zucchini are used to make this quick and simple frittata. This meal is guilt-free because each serving only contains 115 calories.

Total Time: Twenty five minutes

Servings: Four

Ingredients

- One cup refrigerated or frozen egg product, thawed or 4 eggs
- Half cup finely shredded reduced-fat cheddar cheese
- Two tablespoons snipped fresh flat-leaf parsley
- ¼ teaspoon ground black pepper
- 1/8 teaspoon salt
- Two teaspoons olive oil
- Twelve ounces zucchini, halved lengthwise and sliced
- Four green onions, sliced

Directions

- ❖ A rack should be placed in the top third of the oven, which should be heated to 450 degrees F. Whisk the eggs, cheese, pepper, salt, and half the parsley in a medium bowl. Place aside.

- ❖ Warm up the olive oil in a 9- to 10-inch ovenproof skillet over medium-high heat. Green onions and zucchini should be added. Cook for 5 to 8 minutes, stirring frequently, or until just tender.

- ❖ Pour the egg mixture over the vegetables with caution. heat to a medium setting. Run a spatula around the edge of the skillet as the mixture sets, lifting the egg mixture so the uncooked portion flows beneath. Up until the egg mixture is nearly set, cook and lift the edges for an additional 5 minutes (surface will be moist). If necessary, turn down the heat to avoid overbrowning.

❖ In the oven, put the skillet. Bake the frittata for about 5 minutes, or until it is firm and golden on top. Add the final 2 tablespoons of parsley. wedges should be cut. Serve hot

Avocado Hummus

It's so simple to make this vibrant green hummus; just throw a few ingredients in the food processor and pulse! This healthy dip is made with avocado and aquafaba (the chickpea can's liquid).

extra creamy and smooth. Serve with crudités, pita chips, or vegetable chips.

Total Time: Ten minutes

Servings: Ten

Ingredients

- One (15 ounce) can no-salt-added chickpeas
- One ripe avocado, halved and pitted
- One cup fresh cilantro leaves
- ¼ cup tahini
- ¼ cup extra-virgin olive oil
- ¼ cup lemon juice
- One clove garlic

- One teaspoon ground cumin
- Half teaspoon salt

Directions

- ❖ Chickpeas should be drained, with 2 tablespoons of the liquid saved. Add the chickpeas and the liquid you set aside to a food processor.
- ❖ Avocado, cilantro, tahini, oil, lemon juice, garlic, cumin, and salt should all be added. until very smooth, puree. Serve with crudités, pita chips, or vegetable chips.

Gingerbread Tea Cake

Molasses, cinnamon, ginger, and ground cloves give this low-calorie cake its festive flavor. During the holidays, serve it as dessert.

Total Time: One hour

Servings: Thirty five

Ingredients

- Three cups all-purpose flour
- Two teaspoons baking powder
- One teaspoon ground ginger
- One teaspoon ground cinnamon
- Half teaspoon baking soda
- ¼ teaspoon salt
- ¼ teaspoon ground cloves
- Half cup canola oil
- ¼ cup granulated sugar or sugar substitute blend equivalent to 1/4 cup sugar (see Tip)
- Two cups cold water
- 2/3 cup full-flavor molasses

- Half cup refrigerated or frozen egg product, thawed, or 2 eggs, lightly beaten
- Fresh raspberries for garnish

Directions

- ❖ Set oven to 350 degrees Fahrenheit. Prepare a baking pan measuring 13x9x2 inches by lightly spraying it with nonstick cooking spray.
- ❖ Flour, baking powder, ginger, cinnamon, baking soda, salt, and cloves should all be combined in a medium bowl and set aside.
- ❖ Oil and sugar should be combined by whisking them together in a big bowl. Whisk in the eggs, molasses, and cold water after adding them.

- ❖ All at once, whisk in the reserved flour mixture with the water mixture. Fill prepared pan with liquid.
- ❖ A wooden toothpick inserted close to the center should come out clean after 40 to 45 minutes of baking.
- ❖ Totally cool on a wire rack. If desired, top with confectioners' sugar and garnish with raspberries.

Conclusion

Maintaining a proper vegetarian diet can help you control your blood sugar. Consult a dietician to help you create the ideal vegetarian diet plan and to learn how to stick to it.

Pregnant women and people with diabetes can both safely eat vegetarian. It is essential to speak with a dietician before making dietary changes. It guarantees a balanced diet and helps you avoid hypoglycemic episodes. You receive advice from a dietician regarding the ideal carbohydrate intake to prevent high or low blood sugar.

Here are some advice for diabetics who follow a vegetarian diet:

- ❖ Eat a variety of sugar-controlling fruits, vegetables, and nuts to satisfy your body's nutritional requirements.
- ❖ Count the number of carbohydrates you consume at each meal. Make sure to spread

out your daily carbohydrate intake.

❖ As soon as you begin the vegetarian diet for diabetes, keep an eye on your blood glucose levels. Diabetes patients will benefit from appropriately adjusting their medication and insulin dosage.

❖ Patients with diabetes should avoid refined grains like rice and lentils, refined sugar, potatoes, processed foods, and fried foods. Patients with diabetes should keep an eye out for these foods.

❖ Additionally, speaking with a dietician is important. According to a diabetic patient's age, lifestyle, blood sugar levels, and other medical conditions, a dietician makes sure to offer the best diet plan and vegetarian recipes.